Would you like to be more informed and inspired?

Lifejoy is a unique experience of uplifting

motivation and realistic resilience.

If you want to be fortified with compassion and contribution

~Lifejoy is for you!

First published in Great Britain in 2013 by
Rebecca Williams Dinsdale

ISBN: 978-0-9575589-2-2

Printed by Biddles, part of the MPG Books Group

Dr Rebecca Williams Dinsdale is the founder of Lifejoy. She works to inspire your resilience through Lifejoy Lectures and workshops. She is an expert in adversity because she has had so much of it! Rebecca understands the tremendous challenges presented with severe physical illness. She has had between 12-40 weeks a year in bed or hospital for 19 years yet managed to find her Lifejoy tools to help her gain 'A' levels, a prize winning degree, a distinction at Master's level and a PhD. Throughout these very challenging years there were moments of great hope, warmth and humour. Ask her about the bedroom window, the Micra's battery and the fire escape! Dr Rebecca is now self-employed as a professional speaker and writer which has been the wisest use of her experiences and energy! In addition, she is a mentor to new businesses, patron of Sunderland Headlight and a Lay-Preacher in the Church of England (with a very liberal and inclusive attitude). She hopes to help you find more joy through being more motivated, organised and resilient.

So what would you do if all your life stopped at the age of 17 or 27 or 57? If you have hit an obstacle in your life or work then you need the Lifejoy tools to help you find a way through. If you are doing well and would like just a little more hope or direction then Lifejoy will also fit you beautifully. Lifejoy will help you enhance your attitudes and values to shine more brightly. Let's work together so that we aren't defined by our circumstances, let's be defined by our character and courage. Please read the reassuring testimonials and for your resilience to be inspired book Dr Rebecca for a Lifejoy Keynote Lecture, Lifejoy Group Training or Lifejoy Individual Coaching session and see the improvement to your daily life.

Call 0191 5843941 or 0750 4815638 or contact me at www.lifejoy.co

# Acknowledgements

Thank you to my editor, example and enabler.

To our friends who visited,
your loyalty has been love itself.

To all the bravest souls with Severe M.E., for those by their side and the informed medics and Biomedical Researchers who keep trying for them. We salute your courage, integrity and resilience.

Always to Marion, Nigel and Kevin,
who are my joy, example and purpose.

# Contents

# Lifejoy Meditation

Lifejoy is a philosophy of living in hopeful resilience. Whatever happens in our lives we can still strive to reach our potential in the fullest kind of faith, hope and love. Life's joys are waiting for us: sometimes when we least expect them, sometimes after a long slog to the top of challenge. To keep searching for meaningful hope when things look bleak demands the greatest levels of courageous trust, yet there are countless times when our work and waiting are rewarded. In those rare moments when we see snatches of greatness we glimpse heaven on earth.

It is important to remember that we can define our own meanings of greatness which allows us a wonderful level of liberation. When we are realistic about our own positions and make wise decisions then we are laying the foundations for  success. We need to work towards an attitude and a set of actions that are consistently applied in our daily lives.

Gratitude and fortitude are the tools for our trip. In between the challenges of life, God's plan for us is to feel joy. Yet all this sounds great in theory but how do we attain such joy? Well, working to have a good heart and happy hours is all about effort ~ planning, preparation and action and this book will help you be a little bit more organised, reassured and productive.

Having spent the last year sharing the Lifejoy philosophy, tools and strategies with thousands of people, there were many requests to have some form of written support. Meeting such tremendous souls helped to evolve my material so that Lifejoy Lectures, Training and Coaching sessions were as fit for purpose as possible. After reading many self help and development books I came to the conclusion that they were all voices in the wider conversation of life. I hope that this book is one such a voice where spirituality and motivation cooperate to make the most of our experiences. I made a deliberate decision not to write masses of prose or tax the reader too much because we live in busy times with many people under great stress. This is a book that you can dip into, read in any order or pick at a certain part to suit your circumstances. It starts at the very beginning of this day and helps you navigate through the changing seasons of our lives. It is neither comprehensive nor exhaustive in its content, it's just a contribution for your journey. There is a blend of prayers, meditations and exercises to help you think and pray about your life. Self knowledge is a wonderfully helpful tool in navigating your path. By completing the easy tasks and exercises, they will help you see who you are, what you love and what you have. This is meant to be a fun, intriguing and insightful experience to lead you to flourish and bloom further. So find your favourite pen and get ready to love your lists!

This is the culmination of much searching, yearning and learning. It was written in the hope that it would uplift, reassure and inspire. When I introduce myself to a large audience I often say that I am expert in adversity because I have had so much of it! There has been hurt, illness and difficulty in my life, yet throughout the muddle, I know that God has got hold of us and will not let go. My hope, belief and knowledge of this fact has been furnished with evidence from the most magnificent people and I can still feel the most immense excitement and wonder at the wealth of normality that is available to us. In all of this Lifejoy philosophy I have written what I need to learn most. I have more questions than answers and more doubts than certainties yet my quest for Lifejoy remains a daily duty. Thank you for picking up this little offering, let's travel together in hope, in faith and pray for joy to light the way. Let's move safely with a smile and an arm outstretched. Resurrection joy is waiting. Go well my friend.

# Lifejoy

Can you feel it?
Do you live it?
Close your eyes.
Go inside.
Just be.
Imagine.
All is growth.
Embrace change.
Rejoice to reassure.
Be the spark.
Name your joy.
Go to it.
Truly live.

# A Letter to Myself

This is a surprisingly revealing exercise and can be done at any age. If you're cracking on a bit, then write it to your younger self. If you're still a young pup, then it's a wonderful way to start to think about who you would like to become and how you will get there. At 38 years old as I write this, I might be bang in the middle, so I thought I would do the younger self. My effort is included to help you see that this is an easy thing to do. You may cry, laugh and be gently comforted by what comes out. It will probably include similar lines such as, 'don't worry', 'it will work out', 'keep going', 'you were right', 'you were wrong', 'you will survive and thrive still.'

So go on, get thinking and start doing!

## Darling Becca,

You are doing really well, more than enough. Your warmth and initiative shine through and far more people love you than you will ever realise. Mummy and Daddy do everything in order to protect and provide for you. Their whole lives are centred on your well-being. Jobs applied for and got or turned down; houses bought or not; offers taken or not ~ each decision rested on upon the question ~ How will that affect our beloved Becca? That is the best start that you could have had in life to be planned and wanted so much. Granny and Auntie Bet send endless letters talking about you. When Mummy and Daddy are disciplining you it is then that they love you the most. In time, you will see that you will agree with all they said and that keeping you safe was their job. They worried about you with every breath, challenge and bump.

Being pretty and thin are really second best to being brave, wise and kind. You are slim enough and look fit and well. But remember your body is your best friend and you must take better care of yourself. Your health is more fragile than other little ones so be careful. Rest and sleep more. Save a bit of energy for later, throwing yourself into every single thing will exhaust your soul. Learn to observe and savour more. Don't worry about what will come in your school reports. Those who are insightful will see what matters and the rest don't matter. Ironic turnarounds will occur and God's grace will see you through. The Divine sense of humour will travel with you as you turn all those corners. Going to school with Dad was really the best decision.

Stop trying so hard to please. You are quite enough as you are. Not everything is your responsibility or for you to fix. Leave something for someone else to do. Well done for not joining in with the crowd but you don't have to prove it to such a detrimental level. Saying no was very wise to the smoking, drinking and boys ~ well done. Wise boundaries allow for true trust to develop. Deep romance and astonishing adventures are waiting, I promise. It will be more than you could ask or imagine. You will think to yourself, "you couldn't make this up" on repeated occasions.

Now through all that illness hold firm to Jesus. He has got hold of you. Hold on darling, because this is going to last longer and be harder than anyone will tell you. But everyone does see your effort and smile. Keep looking for good and growth and know that all in the end is harvest. Everything will become clear. Your wise planning will be rewarded. Your decisions have been the best you could have made at the time with the information available. The writing and speaking will bear much fruit in unexpected ways. All that Oprah and inspirational stuff will pay off. Research, experience and qualification are always valuable. Tortoises and hares rarely finish together, there will be much delayed gratification, too much toil and things will make no sense. But sense comes in the end with blessings and your kind of peace. Seasons and stages in life will come and go. There will be days when you will be thankful that you have survived long enough to get through and there will be days that you never want to end. These are the extremes of a life well lived, so embrace the richness of the middle ground of ordinary hours. Keep at it darling. Negotiate and navigate your way through with your usual grace, good humour and guts. Just because you're well will not necessarily mean all is well. Minds, Bodies and Souls need Trinitarian investment and care.

Mum wanted everything to be easy for you. When it wasn't she was pained and if loving you would have fixed everything then you would be sorted. All that visiting was worth it. She appreciated it more than words can describe. Stephen has been right by his boy and has stayed at his side through the darkest times. His light is recognised and rewarded in his presence for you.

As the song says, "Strength, courage and wisdom are all inside of me" ~ they are in you my beauty. Believe, know and do. Will it be easy? No. Will it be worthwhile, exciting, challenging? Absolutely. Grow more into yourself and gather those around you. Your Lifejoy is always calling and wonderful things await.

So having read my offering, how did it make

you feel? A little bit better, I hope. The themes are universal and with a little empathy and imagination can mould something to fit you perfectly.   It was a demanding   to write, reassuring to read and always available for consultation, editing   and additions ~ just like our lives. If you're unsure about how to proceed then there is another option that might be easier to tackle. What about thinking about your ideal eulogy? What would you like someone to say about you at the end of your days?

I did it many years ago and it set the plan for my life up beautifully. It wasn't a grand wish list but stated the landmarks of achievement in terms of relationships and activities I hoped I would manage. The most important part of it was that it talked about the values I had lived out, the joy experienced and the challenges that survived. Sometimes I look over it to check myself and realise that I have missed some of the big things out. It is an evolving document and I know that buying a bright yellow camper van and driving it to Cornwall to go surfing was out of my capacity in my 20's but there is time yet! Now I am approaching 40 there has been a realisation that I am just too long to fit into a camper van so a little caravan with a kind bald man seems a much more practical and lovely option. Being in that caravan with the people I love makes me feel most alive. What make's you feel alive? How can you adapt the ideal to fit with your circumstances? It may take you ten years to get to it but just the seed of an idea can generate great things. And just as I write this, the radio has just started to play the tune "Young at Heart" ~ think that must be a sign to spur us on!

Now that we have made a start on ourselves, it's time for the first of our wonderlists. When we are building our truest selves it helps if we have a CV for our souls. One of the messages that came from my clients whilst working with Lifejoy Coaching was that we need to transfer the best of our professional lives into our personal lives and vice-versa. There are well known measures to assess our performance in the working world which are really helpful for our life at home as well. The SWOT and PEASE tests are often used to assess the current state of things for a business or institution. The following are warmer versions which will trigger happy memories and make you realise just how much you really have. Make a list under the following titles. If it's a bit thin, then that is telling you to go and make some new memories because your best is yet to come! Take a little time to think about your answers and enjoy this exercise because it's a win-win!

# The Joy of Making a Good List!

The most loving people in my life are

_____

_____

_____

_____

Whom must I thank? Did you have an amazing teacher, neighbour or club leader who encouraged you?

_____

_____

_____

_____

With whom must I spend more time?

_____

_____

_____

_____

# My Life Timetable

By this time next year I would like to:

_____

_____

_____

_____

In three years time I would like to:

_____

_____

_____

_____

In five years time I would like to:

_____

_____

_____

_____

If you're stuck for answers, then think about your possible answers in the context of the following things ~ your location, position, finances, relationships, health, travels and holidays, education, training and qualifications, spirituality and hobbies ~ anything that really excites or stimulates you. What makes your eyes light up and your heart race at the thought of doing? It might take a while and a bit of planning but there might come a time when everything is in place for you to embark on your desired course. Most importantly you need to know that course and be able to visualise yourself feeling the joy they deliver. Once you know that, you can start planning and practising.

# The Worth of Our Values …

Lifejoy is about values; the values we all need to live productive and peaceful lives. Lifejoy works to enable self-discipline, organisation and enthusiasm. Lifejoy promotes courage, wisdom, manners, trust and truth. Good values are one of those commodities where the more you have the better! Once you have the Lifejoy bug it starts to become part of you and something of a joyful duty to apply those values as widely and diligently as possible. Most of us would appreciate more joy, order, determination and discipline in our lives and finding out who we are and where we would like to be are essential to our growth. Whatever has happened in our lives, we can hope to evolve through our thinking, our language and our actions. We are not the labels we give ourselves, we are not the worst thing we have done, neither are we the best. We are somewhere in the middle and always striving for a balance. We are neither the dysfunction whence we came nor are we the dysfunction in which we may be in the middle of at this moment. As the young writer, Zadie Smith said, "You are never stronger than when you have landed on the other side of despair." Sir Winston Churchill said, "Success is not final, failure is not fatal; it is the courage to continue that counts." The continued application of honourable values in our daily dialogues, deliberations and deliveries leads to creating the space for hope to become manifest. One of my favourite Biblical quotes is, "God did not send us into the world in timidity, but in a spirit of love, power and self-discipline." As we are fortified by these lovely quotes, let's press onwards and upwards.

Here are some of the most honourable characteristics, attitudes and values. It's wise to think about how they are applied in our lives and how we can increase them.

There are spaces for you to fill in at the end of the list. Think about what matters to you the most and how that can be described as your values. Here are some of the best to get you started …

- Truth
- Fairness
- Altruism
- Wisdom
- Kindness

- Trust
- Love
- Hope
- Courage
- Faith
- Compassion
- Forgiveness
- Reliability
- Altruism
- Joy
- Reliability
- Initiative
- Gratitude
- Determination
- Organisation
- Enthusiasm
- Self-Discipline

Lots of people think about the values they most desire in other people. Maybe it would be good thing to propagate them in ourselves first and that might just do the trick in attracting the right kind of people into our lives. If we wish to have loving fulfilling relationships with reliable fun people then we must first present those attributes in ourselves. When we can align the values in ourselves with those in the people around us, we bind our souls together which makes society stronger and our world a better place. So which values do your behaviour best demonstrate and why? Which values would you like to develop further? What do you value most in other people?

In myself ...

_____
_____
_____
_____

In others ...

_____
_____
_____
_____

How well do these correlate? What can I do to help them to correlate?

_____
_____
_____
_____

# Quality Questions
# Make Quality Lives ...

Now that we have looked at our values it's wise to look at how we hold ourselves to account for their implementation. Little children and often some grown-up ones, often ask the question, "Why?" Sometimes it is the most powerful question we can ask of ourselves and our situations and sometimes it is the most pointless. It is powerful when we have some control over our circumstances and it is pointless when we are doing all we can and have to realise that we are not superhuman and cannot control everything. If we consistently make the best decisions with the best knowledge we have at the time then we are doing all that we can. Within those experiences there will be many times when the following questions will help us to do the best that we can within the constraint of our challenges. Some of these questions are quite demanding so don't worry if you can't answer them all at once. I still struggle with them but if we keep trying and learning together then great things are possible.

- What am I doing to make it better?
- How am I contributing to this situation or relationship?
- What should I be doing that I know I am putting off?
- How can I make progress today?
- Why am I procrastinating?
- Do I need more information to make a wise decision?
- Is it wise to proceed?
- Should I pause, press on or pull out?
- What does the evidence tell me?

The final question, "What does the evidence tell me?" is one that Historians are frequently asking themselves. As we move from our history to our present and future, it's time to be greater than the sum of our parts.

# Maths to Relish and Cherish Your Life

Being good at sums and using your IQ isn't something that we should leave to the brainy people. There is a significant difference between being intelligent, educated and sensible. When we can manage to combine these three assets we set ourselves up to be our best selves. Living well takes wit, mental dexterity and humility. So how can we make the sums in our lives relevant to cherishing our opportunities? My Father is a mathematician and often says that a good solution is elegant and that everything can be reduced to an equation. He also frequently draws graphs to explain complex things to us and warns about too much debt and the power of inflation. It would be easy to think that managing our money is one of the only areas where mathematics is present in our adult life. Well it's about time we expanded its role so that we can all benefit from understanding a good graph or compound interest. A good way to start is with a simple equation which is based on fulfilling our potential.

Efficiency + Effectiveness
= Excellence

Good Process + Good People
= Optimal Outcomes

Being organised and optimistic are the foundations for optimal outcomes. Having self-discipline to do the very best job we can points us to our brilliance. We can't pretend that good fortune and good genetics don't play a significant role in our lives. Nevertheless there are things that we can control which are in our equations above.

The word geometry comes from the Greek, Geo, which means earth and measure. Triangles have a Trinitarian beauty within, so I thought they were the best way to display how the foundations of our lives are composed. When we are able to recognise these structures then we are able to align them and live consistently within the values we most appreciate.

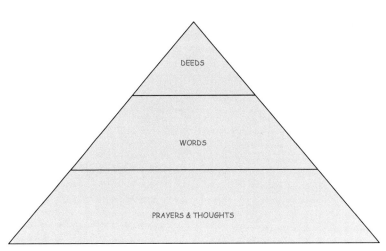

A good diagram can sometimes be more effective than a thousand words. Having understood that our prayers, thoughts, words and deeds are built upon one another, we can progress to see that our attitudes, aims and actions all flow in a circular direction. They are inter-dependent and reinforce one another. The most important thing is to make sure that they are all healthy and we strive to keep a balance in our lives.

Attitudes

Aims

Actions

# Your Life's Script

What are you doing with the grand gift of your life?
How are you using your hours, talents and tales?
If it were to stop tomorrow,
would you have used all your potential?
Or have a tank full of creativity and contribution left?
Today is the day to take it on.
What would you do if you couldn't fail?
What do you love? Is it offered in service?
Go quiet and make a list with a target for each day.
A dream is merely a goal with a timeline.
No more excuses, you know what to do. Now do it.
This is a once run thing and God is waiting,
to watch you fly. or run, or just be.
The great blessing of your life is to use your potential.
What are you doing with your grand gift of life?

# Getting to Know Myself

My favourite colour is    _____

My favourite place is     _____

My favourite song is      _____

My favourite book is      _____

My favourite film is      _____

My favourite music is     _____

My role models are        _____


My ideal day would be

_____

_____

_____

_____

# Fantastic Things to Do

Play
Apologise.
Volunteer
Declutter
Give Blood
Go to Church
Always use Gift Aid
Go to a night class or college course
Sign up for the Organ Donor Register
Pledge a small amount (or large) of money
each month to a charity
Recycle, reuse, reduce your consumption
Try something completely new
Take a deep breath
Join a club or choir
Reach out
Sit still
Smile
Read
Pray

# What Are You Doing to Make it Better?

Whenever I have set out to write a book, there has been a clear and determined plan about what kind of material would emerge. Then the most interesting thing happened. I did the research, kept to the plan and started to type and something completely different emerged. It was as if I were expecting to produce an apple and came out with an orange ~ still fruit but an entirely different colour and composition. This book was just the same and I realised that my branding for this entity was different from the self-help / life-coaching book I intended to write. I desperately didn't want it to be saccharine or sentimental, yet consistently the themes of discipline, manners, courage and hard work permeated every sentence. Overriding optimism or pessimism lack much sense about them whereas HOPE, ENDEAVOUR and COURAGE are a mighty trio. They are the tools with which to interact with ourselves, our life and our world.

In a world where the news is dominated by bad things ~ stabbings, disasters, conflict, intense poverty and corruption, I had to question my intentions and hopes for this book. It wasn't meant to be a jolly little read where it stroked you for a while and made no lasting effect on things. The realisation that perhaps if there were more manners, values and courage then we could dramatically alter what we see in the media. It would be easy to sink into despair when there is so much disease, degeneration and disloyalty everywhere. The best antidote to all these problems is **discipline** ~ to have the discipline to live as healthily as possible, to keep learning and remain loyal. My father was a headmaster and being the headmaster's daughter never leaves you, neither does the discipline! He once said to me that the more "discipline there is, the more freedom you have" which I think that meant that when you say no to a child, that no means no and you have to be consistent with them and with yourself. It's so easy to feel overwhelmed in a world facing so many challenges on so many fronts but the message of this book is that one person's efforts are as valuable as a thousand. This was beautifully illustrated to me one day when I was in the middle of a great and enduring challenge in my life. I came across a film about the life of the South African, Steve Biko, who was fighting against the appalling evils of apartheid. In the film, the journalist who wrote the book about Steve Biko's life said to his wife,

*"We have got to do something and this is what I can do."*

And what he could do, was to write the book and let the world know what was going on in South Africa. This leads us to the question about, "What can we do to make it better?" The only answers we can proffer are to know yourself, grow yourself and from that, give of yourself. Give in a tiny way every day whether that be a smile, opening a door, standing up for someone, or making a positive choice in a negative situation.

The first positive choice in a negative situation is one of the most powerful options in the world. Sometimes the only thing we can manage is to keep going, ask for help or accept that we have done all we can.

# The Way of the World

The outer experience is a mere reflection
of your perception and inner reality.
Are you a giver or a taker or somewhere in between?
It's not your fault yet responsibility awakens in you
to toil and speak to make it just.
Do you buy "fair-trade" or sponsor a little one with no
shoes, or listen to a hurting soul when their troubles are
loud?
Great dramas will unfold with tragedy, disaster and attack.
Our response is the measure of our humanity and courage.
A special need is a special gift so thank the good Lord that
He showed us the way.
Discipline and manners mend much, so much.
Where outer glory shines from within.

# Money

Cash is energy so with it respect its power and
potential to make things fair, kind or bold.
Never waste or hoard or fear.
Save enough, give enough, be enough.
So that you are defined by who you are,
not what you have accumulated.
Be the first to offer to pay, sponsor or tithe.
What goes around, comes around in cash, like or form.
So stop the tick or loans for stuff that sits to dust.
When in doubt, just recall the millions who would swap.
Let's use our energy well to savour true wealth.

# Family Meditation

To live in a spirit of Lifejoy, the first step is to appreciate what we already have. The basis of a family unit is a rich foundation and it stays with us all of our lives. Whatever the permutation of that grouping, however unconventional ~ all that really matters is that we have someone in the world who loves us. That's all anyone ever wants or needs. When we hear about terrible cases of abuse, neglect or indifferent parenting we can only thank God if we had been spared such hurt. For those who weren't spared such an experience, then we send you all our love and hope that you were able to rebuild yourself for happier times ahead. Whatever has happened, there is always the chance to be that which we most desire. When Mothering Sunday or Father's Day comes around, there is probably a number of people who have been instrumental in our nurturing who need a 'thank you' and a hug. Indeed, as adults we still carry our childhoods with us and need to keep nurturing ourselves and each other. Culturally we are enticed into thinking that romantic love will fix everything. To have a fairytale wedding is seen as the best day of our life. For many, it is a great blessing but it is crucial to realise the strength of all the relationships in our lives. In whatever form to be able to say to someone  ~ I did love you, I do love you and I will love you ~ creates the kind of unity on earth that is heaven sent. Why not draw yourself your own team tree?

# Friends and Family Tree

The following prayers are to help you see what you have and maybe to tell someone how valuable they are to you.

# For My Parent

I thank God for you, my friend,
my example and my helper.
Thank you for being mine.
I love you. Thank you for loving me so well.
I endeavour to be all that you have instilled in me
and let my light shine for your warmth and way.
I am sorry I worried and grieved you.
I understand now, you knew more of the world.
Now I see your wisdom.
The gift of my life was to start it with you.
The purpose of my life is continue by your side.
I thank God for you, my friend.

# A Brother

This is the privilege of your life,
to guard, to guide, to be a pal and a blessing to your brother.
Set an example of being loyal to your parents and friends.
Show that you can be trusted to care, grow and give.
In a spirit of fun and togetherness keep patient and share.
Your temper can be held and your words must be wise.
Keep the challenges in mind whilst reaching for adventure.
Race to be the first to stand up and be counted
at your brother's side as a man and a friend.

# A Sister

A sister is a sacred thing to share and protect.
Set an example and be the one
who shines enough to show what can be done and how
to live with vigour and purpose.
When inevitable challenges come, be at your sister's
side, to listen, enable and encourage.
She is the treasure that will always be yours,
a little soul in your charge for the rest of your lives.
Grow together as friends.
Being family takes work, grace and God in your hearts.
Being a sister is a sacred gift.

# My Friend

Thank you for the immense gift of yourself,
for being by my side, inspiring and uplifting.
I have so enjoyed our laughter and talks.
My soul is richer because of you.
You have been joyous, reliabile and
caring, always sweet tempered and gracious.
Thank you for being pleased for me
when things went well and for
being by my side when troubles hit.
May you know a thousand,
thousand blessings, see hope in the
eyes of others, feel wonder of all kinds
and know at the deepest level,
you are my family.

# My Beloved

Thank you for holding my soul,
safe and well in your heart.
I cherish your company
through our journeying together.
May your dreams be manifested in us?
You are all for which I hoped and more.
May I be so for you?
When you slip, I will reach out,
as you do for me.
Your hand is all I need.
Always at my side,
I adore you.

# For Getting Married

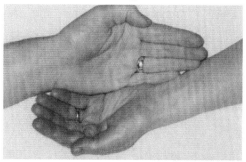

Your true growth starts today,
forgive and  compromise
as understanding makes peace and joy bloom.
Your challenges will show where you need to grow.
Hold your minds together and walk in the light of love
and then natural romance will flow
as bins are emptied and the fridge is filled.
You are the safest home for each other.
Make time, be thoughtful and kind.
Behave as well as you can.
Keep remembering the best.
Say 'I'm sorry,'  'I don't know,'
'I would like,' and 'What do you think?'
Make your marriage be defined by,
'I Love You' and 'Thank you.'

# A Meditation on Your Beliefs

Are you brave enough to believe? Are you? Go on, I know you want to…. Before we go any further it's important to examine exactly what we do believe because beliefs are our anchors that need careful maintenance. If we have sensible empowering beliefs then it is highly likely that we will have sensible empowering lives. If you believe the world is out to get you and that everyone is mean and selfish then that is very likely to produce those kinds of experiences. What you believe may have been shaped by your experience or by other people. So today is the day to think through what you would like to believe and to start taking responsibility for implementing those ideals into new positive patterns in your life. Beliefs can build, break or bother us throughout our lives. Our daily experiences come around to teach us to see what is happening within ourselves. So make the grand decision not to tell any more sad stories about how you were done down or how it wasn't your fault. It may not have been your fault but it is your responsibility to pick up the pieces and build something better for yourself.

Once we recognise the patterns that are self-defeating then we can stand back from them and do something in a new way. It might just be that you are a wonderfully rounded soul with pristine beliefs that need no work at all, maybe just the odd polish. Otherwise, if you're like me and most other people it is good to realise that if we keep having the same unwelcome results or situation occur in our lives then we must do something differently to produce a better outcome.  This must be one of the most powerful ways to move towards having more joy. Time for another lovely list, take a little bit of time and use the insights to grow in strength.

Formerly I believed in

_____

_____

I believed that I am

_____

_____

I believed that my role in life is to

_____

_____

I believed that the world is

_____

_____


In future I believed that people are

_____

_____

In future I choose to believe that I am

_____

_____

I now choose to believe that I
can influence my role in life to be

_____

_____

I now choose to believe that the world is

_____

_____

I choose to believe that people are

_____

_____


# I believe, I hope, I trust, I know …

# Your Branding

Lifejoy is about our continued personal development ~ CPD for our minds, hearts and souls. It is about building our truest treasures from within and letting them shine out to our world. Of course, this is a little borrowing from the marvellous concept of Continuing Professional Development where employees are expected to keep learning and growing as professionals. My husband gets very enthused about the whole concept of ongoing learning and training. His CPD file is a tremendous sight to behold. Another place with which I have great affection is the University of Sunderland, where there is the wonderful slogan of, 'Lifelong Learning.' When I started my studies with them there was a television advert which called us to, 'Move on Up!' I loved that thought. Everyone accepts that we need to plan and prepare well for our working lives but we need to put as much effort into our personal lives which are the bedrock for our working efforts. With all this Lifejoy effort it's important to make sure that we market ourselves in the most effective and efficient manner. At its best, marketing has a moral basis and isn't just about selling us more stuff that we don't really need. A good product or person offers to enhance our lives with the results that their presence brings. This process is called "added value" and is the holy grail of sustainable selling. There is also a well-known  concept about the 4P's ~ product, price, promotion, placing ~ so what is your brand? Are you valuing yourself enough? How are you presented? Do you look and feel your best? Are you putting yourself in the best of environments with good people around you? Are you learning, loving and living to the best that you can manage?

In this Lifejoy journey into growth and knowledge we are working to appreciate and enhance every element of ourselves. The crucial outcome from this process is to reap the rewards of improved personal and professional judgement ~ to make sensible and sustainable choices that generate deep and reliable relationships and experiences. And what you need internally and externally is an inner surety which is based on sincere confidence.

# Confidence

To shine with self acceptance, confidence and a genuine warmth is something to which we can all work. To have outer confidence needs a sure foundation inside, to enable our thoughts to align to our words and deeds. Being aware of the parts of ourselves that produce negative situations or feelings is the first stage of growth. Once we know what the issues are then we have the choice to learn something new and make something new. We must be aware of our internal chatter and how we think of ourselves. To speak to yourself in the same way we would to the person we love most in the world is a kind and productive way to start. Apart from God, the only person you can guarantee having a life-long relationship with is ourself, thus it would be wise to make it as good a relationship as possible.

Often the most socially capable people have merely learned methods to cope and master their communication. Having a little list of potential topics of conversation ready is a good move. People really enjoy talking about themselves so asking several questions and then listening with attention and interest will help steer through new situations. By asking open-ended general questions or merely introducing yourself with a compliment can be a tremendous social lever. A mere smile is a great asset alongside being gracious and pleased for the success of others. Having the self-confidence not to boast about your own achievements whilst also being self-assured enough to share your talents is a delicate balance. Most people will respond well and the more we practise then the better our skills will become. Positive body language, good eye contact, clear diction and good posture do a lot to enable our cohesion.

Whatever our social and communication skills, we are all under some pressure to conform and feel accepted. How much we adhere to this norm is within our choice. How we look, what we say, how we live our lives is all within our control. We must value the things that matter and not be pushed by consumerism to conform. Whatever our size, shape, age or appearance delivers to us, we need to remember that there will always be people who are better looking, younger, fitter and generally stunning people around us. There will also be people who would long to look like you, be like you or have your abilities and talents. Beauty is indeed, in the eye of the beholder. Some of the most beautiful and capable people I admire are not conventionally attractive, yet there is something about their inner light that shines with a warmth and wit that is wondrous. The blessing of growing older is that we have gathered a great deal of experience and knowledge; this then empowers the soul into its most vibrant impact. Focussing on the best parts of ourselves, working on the rest and enjoying our age are the most sensible ways to make peace with our imperfections. With true confidence our capabilities and courage are amplified. Then our initial contribution is to be the best that we can be and then we should offer it out to the world and value the wonders that may return to us.

Now remember what we said about fitting in? Well, this must be one of the most pressing issues for many of us!

# No Marriage, No Kids Yet?

So then, you'd dared to be with yourself in full glow, released from pressures and pushes to have options that those conformers may never taste.
Being independent, solo or cohabiting all lodge comfortably in our world.
You have a unique special slot where it all still might happen.
Be aware, give, get out and see all that you can do and be.
Cherish controlling your destiny, your way and your time.
The smug people aren't always as successful as they seem.
Some of them might even swap!
Be glad, whatever.

Considering the last offering, it might seem a little strange that we are about to focus on the marvels of having a child. Whether or not we are a parent, we've been a child so let's read these pieces with grateful hearts from where we have come or what we may yet experience. The glory of the human trajectory is about to unfold for you …

# My Baby

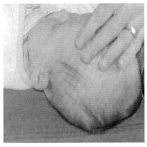

From the first thought of you when God formed
your bones in the depth of my being;
I had a pure hope.
Now I know my own Mother, as new.
Our connection eternally stronger
as we were knit together.
We all are growing into our most
magnificent selves, into all the grand potential
and beyond anything that I could imagine.
May God bless your every breath and step
as I feel your presence in the essence of my being.
I am for you. I brace myself
for equal measure of pride, worry
and delight in you. You are the best
evidence of God, Divine's greatest gift to me.
In deepest gratitude, always,
always know ~ I love you.

# My Child

Thank God for the miracle of you.
Your care is the purpose of my life.
You will never know how much I love
every part of you and beyond.
I pray for you with every breath for safety, joy
and grace to embrace your every minute.
With whatever help you need,
I will work to enable or step back.
Through discipline and example
I love you most, in preparation
for the spectrum of all experiences.
Please know I will never leave
your side in body, mind and spirit.
In awe, I see your progress and courage.
I learn from you in praise of what God has given.
Thank heaven for sending me you.

# For Working Mothers

Hey! Stop for a little minute and see what a
brilliant job you're doing, juggling, planning and
spinning: you are taking care of it all.
Every woman toils whether paid or not,
whilst working to fulfil their potential.
Dispatch the 'oughts' and the 'shoulds,'
hope, believe and know that it's there
for all to see and admire whilst you angst.
Understand that you're at a busy stage of life
when demands feel ceaseless.
Watch, for in a while it will all be done and gone
and you'll wonder where the time went.
So rejoice in the muddle and the mess.
It's God's glory on your floor.
You're doing wonderfully, sleep well ~
Until someone shouts for Mummy!

# For Our Teenager

Embrace your deep beauty and uniqueness
and stand apart to cherish your innocence.
Responsibility will come all too soon.
Use the magnificence of your mind.
Appreciate your health in the fun and the frail.
Realise image and gloss are mere froth, and value
the substance that is in your soul.
Bring to this world your joy, manners and care.
Have courage to set aside those whose behaviour
is not becoming. Be proud to be with your
parents, and always say, I love you.
Choose good friends and be one.
Work hard and be the one who shines.
For the next generation is you. Find your hope,
knowing that you are ours.
Go well my child, go well.

# Leaving Home

The jump to independence is never as it seems.
As with all of life, it's the journey that matters.
So now leap and love and
see what is yet to flourish.
Now you know all that was done in your name and
best interests: it's up to you; yes you.
Suddenly you are alone yet free to develop sound
judgement and good choices.
You'll make mistakes but next time, be better and
grow into the best that you can be.
Gather your legs and brains and soul.
Get going to your future, with a thankful heart for
all that is past and yet to come.
Treat independence as an extension of home.

# Wholesome Vitality

Health in body, mind and spirit is a lifelong endeavour. Constant attention to each area of our well-being is needed to make sure that we can function to our optimum level and enjoy as much of life as possible. Energy is the most precious of commodities and needs to be valued and managed. However much we demand of ourselves there needs to be a reciprocation of care to recharge our batteries.

Many of us do reasonably well in one area and then neglect others and try to fill them with more status, work, possessions or achievements. It never works and leads only to dysfunction and unease. With increasing levels of obesity and depression it seems as if we are over-feeding ourselves in some areas and are undernourished in others. What is so interesting about a balanced effort towards good health is that for some people it is just naturally effortless and for others it is an elusive quest with the occasional success. Wherever we are on this scale, it's important to remember that our efforts really do make a difference to our happiness. Good physical, mental and emotional health are intrinsically linked and reinforcing. The following ideas might help you along a little.

Eat sensibly, move as much as you can, drink lots of water, limit alcohol intake, stop smoking, get enough of both sleep and daylight.

Ask for help, do something you're good at, care for others, accept who you are, take a break, keep in touch, talk about your feelings, keep mentally active. When we are taking care of ourselves in the right way it enables us to start using all of our capacities. In order to utilise them we need a plan …

# My Most Fabulous Plan

I love working with

_____

_____

I am in the flow when I am doing

_____

_____

I am good with

_____

_____

My ideal job would be

_____

_____

Education, qualification, experience I need

_____

_____

Actions I need to start taking to make it
happen today

_____

_____

By the end of this week I will have found out about

_____

_____

By the end of this month I will have done

_____

_____

By the end of this year I will be

_____

_____

# Well Done and Good Luck!

That's the best I can say
for an achievement won so hard.
In admiration and glory we see
your effort, excellence and
empowerment. Now go carefully
with grace to the destiny you
design. In the humility and gratitude
that achieved the success, survey
and surround yourself with all
that is true. For now is your
time to shine in the light of
this grand occasion. Go forward
in confidence and be the next
one who enables another.
Well Done and Good Luck!

# A Good Life is a Balanced Life!

There is currently much emphasis on the ideal work-life balance, yet is it ever really possible to achieve? Well it's the intention that counts and somewhere we will hit a good patch and manage it for a while. Then something might come along that knocks us off course for a while. So here is a structure to help highlight the way to engineer a little bit of daily balance into our lives. Good luck. Don't be afraid to improve this model because we are all learning together!

| MY LIFEJOY | THIS DAY | THIS WEEK | THIS MONTH |
|---|---|---|---|
| JOY | | | |
| GIVING | | | |
| FAMILY | | | |
| FRIENDS | | | |
| PARTNER | | | |

# Your New Job

Congratulations will fly out from
all directions before you start.
Nevertheless, think for a while,
a formidable task awaits.
Power to its last particle is duty, where
responsibility exceeds authority.
Let gallantry and integrity be your guides to
bludgeon any hint of swagger.
When thought or words dare swank of salary,
remember your job is to lead by example,
to equip and enable.
When a need comes for you to bear the
news of another's new job, loss or move; be
constructive, polite and praising of your team.
For it's intentions and efforts that matter.

Tomorrow will dawn with a new demand, debate and drama. Give your all and endeavour to be worthy of your new job.

# My Goals

A good goal is sensible, attainable, and one you enjoy. It can be simple or grand. To manage any big project you need a plan and a mantra. One lovely way to think about it is to do the G>O>D>D process ~ Gratitude, Organisation and Determined Discipline. This manifests itself in your life to being ready to count three blessings each day, get a diary or year planner and build yourself an inspiration wall to keep you determined. Just thinking about what you might like is a really exciting process. The table opposite is to help you organise your thoughts.

|  | In a month | In a year | In three years | In five years |
|---|---|---|---|---|
| Spiritual |  |  |  |  |
| Mental |  |  |  |  |
| Physical |  |  |  |  |

# New Home

The values lived in your home are,
your true North to those you love.
In the bricks and shelves comes
storage for your adventure
into all that maybe wonderful.
It is a sacred space to house your dreams,
which you nurture into being. Your place
to relish new days, lives and living,
It keeps your soul safe between
each layer to your foundations.
May they be sure and sound to
let you dance and breathe and
to be a trinity of blessings
in, of and at home.

# Treasure Box

It's often a good idea to think about the most precious items we possess. If you were given two minutes to grab your most important material possessions, many of us would grab our photographs or items made by our children. In an age where there are the most amazing electronic goods, mobile phones, iPods, televisions on the wall and supercars it is so refreshing to know that of the things we value, most have very little financial worth. I don't think anyone would particularly want to steal or buy my treasures which comprise of a tatty old Bible, a promise box, a collection of letters, journals and a three inch womble with a wonky hat!. Just thinking about which material goods are important to us is an empowering exercise. It makes us focus on what really matters and even though a flashy car, dishwasher and other 'bits of bling' are all very nice, you can't keep them in your pocket or in your heart. Whatever unfolds in our lives we must remember that the first thing we need to grab are our people. Relationships that are supportive and joyful are really the golden threads that bind our lives together.

# The Joy in Your Memories & Hopes

Scrap books and photo albums are the most wonderful things to uplift and reassure. What about making a book that comprises of your best photos, quotes, cards and excerts from letters alongside images of the life you would like? The simple act of seeing and placing the images and words is highly relaxing and restful. We can put together pictures from magazines and words from headlines to form some kind of collage about what we appreciate in our lives and how we can evolve towards our desires. This then acts as a kind of road map to the future with our lists guiding us with the information about our characters and personalities. Some people call these vision or mood boards but we can take that idea further by blending the past, present and future in a compilation of grace, hope and love.

Some of the things we desire won't come our way. The art of being in lifejoy is to realise the blessings which we already have and find ways to accommodate the missing parts. To have it all at once could be too much for us so whatever we're hoping for, may be on its way when we are more prepared to manage it. Go and get your glue and enjoy the process.

# Retirement Liberation!

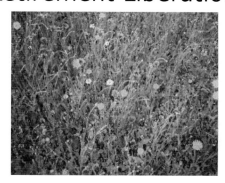

Oh what joy,
you made it to the stage of life
where you can be most yourself
and do all that you love.
Now striving and status have
got you here, use your hours wisely.
Be an elder, giver and grower of minds,
hearts and souls.
Keep embracing ideas, meet people and
explore your world.
Now is the time to get it right.
Test and try to create as much
lasting love as possible.
Oh what joy, you are living it.

# Resilience Meditation

I love courage. It inspires me more than anything. Being brave means being resilient and finding ways through the hard times. It doesn't mean that we aren't fearful, worried or in pain. It just means that we are trying to get up each day and try again. Sometimes courage comes in tiny packages or herculean efforts but we can all grow through challenge and help each other.

Resilience is a skill, an attitude and an emotional muscle. It's grounded in integrity and the drive to come back from whatever has hit us so that we are wiser, stronger and more determined. Super-resilience comes about when someone decides to make something good come from a tragic experience. Such examples are parents who become campaigners after something has happened to their child; people who start charities to support people in similar situations or merely the decision to keep going and keep a loved one's memory alive.

Resilience can also be cultivated through

what many people would call, failure. Everyone seems to be afraid of failing, not getting things right the first time or being flawed. Well, the imperfections of life ensure that we have to manage whatever is sent to us and then what we create is our choice. The following prayers are there to help you through the difficult times. We will all have challenges, pain, worry and fear to some degree throughout our tenure on earth. The more we love then the more likely we are to be vulnerable to such experiences but they are the packaging of joyful times. There will be some lucky people who will look like they are cruising through life without a care or any trouble. And then there will be some people who will have more than their fair share of woes and difficulties. Wherever we are in life, there will always be someone who would swap with us, no matter how bad we feel. Obviously there is the widest range of challenges from major disaster and unexpected grief to frustration and disappointment. It is important to realise that whatever has happened to us, there is a spectrum and that we can slide up or down ~ so we must be aware. There will be seasons and stages where we can't make any sense of anything and the effort to get through each day seems more than we can bear.

Then just at the moment that seems darkest, there will be the tiniest glimmer of kindness, hope or new life. We will hear a tune, see a child or receive some post and that will help us. We may need to pause for a while, catch our breath and crawl before we can walk. It's important to keep our self maintenance up ~ eat enough, sleep more, get fresh air and have a shower. Lots of people say that keeping busy helps and working on a project lets them concentrate on something other than the problem. The oddest things can save us. There was a programme called the "Secret Millionaire" on television which literally stopped me from sinking and the knowledge that at some deep level there is a "Love that wilt not let me go," sent me several lifebelts.

My wonderful Father is the bravest person I have ever encountered. He told me about the latin word, RESURGAM which means, I shall rise again which is very inspiring. We may have to rise many times to survive our situations yet there is always the hope that we can surpass all expectations and thrive as a consequence. To work through trauma, injustice, grief or illness is to do the most important work for our souls. If we can survive then we can thrive. Maybe today is the day when you quietly enable someone else to survive and thrive? Perhaps it will be this hour when you send the card, make the call, reach out a hand and find that you are the lifebelt. Good luck.

# Please Help

I am in a mess and don't know what to do.
There seems only darkness ahead,
yet You are the light.
Please lead me in the way that I should go.
My loved one is hurt and I feel powerless.
Shine Your love on their path and on mine too.
Help, console, direct and renew our spirits so
that we may continue in some form of hope or
muddle to make some good come from this.
Thank you for listening my Lord.
I know You are holding us safe.

# Failure

So what! We had a blip.
Not to worry, just reflect
and listen to learn how to
be better next time. The
sooner it happens the better
for us to see how to improve,
revise and renew. We might
yet look back to see this was
a great blessing. God is always
protecting us from something
worse or preparing us for
something better. Now is the
time to keep at it, don't
dare quit!  Chin up and keep
a good heart. Get going.
Keep going. Go.
Success is in sight.

# A Candle Prayer for You

The light in this candle is sign of my love for you.
The hope in this love is our connection to God.
Where joy is made, honour is earned and compassion
given. Please cherish the chances and choices you have
and be your truest self, so that your light will shine.
If today brings normality you are indeed, blessed.
When the day brings glory, be grateful in your humility.
If today brings challenge, know that you will cope.
However difficult, you can find a way to recover.
Through recovery comes empathy and strength.
Through it all, the courage of Christ
will sustain you. Hold on through the
rough seas, calmer waters are waiting.
The hope in this love is the foundation of life.
The light in this candle is a sign of God's love for us all.

# Homework Always Helps

As the Headmaster's daughter I was always a good girl! Throughout my studies I realised that in wider life, there is an uncomfortable truth that….homework… in whatever capacity it comes, almost always helps a situation. When we're facing a big battle then we need to be prepared. Putting together our case with a logical set of evidence, clear arguments and persistence in putting them across in a calm but firm manner is a good way to approach a demanding situation. In the end it's always about the calibre of material and personnel that are dealing with us. Making notes, practising them out loud and preparing for potential questions will put us in the best possible position for any presentation.

In many respects, homework is really rather like a good sermon! It is organised like this : ~ we need a good argument to convince people, to put it across in a confident but accessible manner and to have a bit a fun in it. One of my staple lines is that "FAITH IS ABOUT VALUES" which is what this book is all about.

The values we need to make good lives and good communities are those which are seen in faith. Looking for inspiration in our Bibles is a wonderful help because all of life is in there ~ all of the great stuff of love, loyalty, labouring and longing alongside all of the things that aren't so good but teach us everything ~ debt, divorce, disaster and death. People from all ages have needed to do their homework and realise the benefits of being prepared and practised. Nevertheless, the central feature of the Christian faith is the hope after death. Therefore, whatever today brings to you, know that the great hope is for you.

# Diagnosis Dropped on You

What a shock, this feels unfair
news to land at your feet.
Recover your standing and
steady yourself to think
about what you can do
to survive and be more
informed. Retain your power,
extend your knowledge to make
as wise a plan as you can.
Effort is never wasted.
In discussion and debate with
relevant parties and experts,
make a list and find the appropriate
research, charities and support.
You'll be doing all you can to make it better.
God's hands will hold you as you pray
to come to a new day as
a stronger, kinder, more faithful soul.
Everything will make sense in the end.

# Rough Waters

I know this is hard for you.
I wish I could fix it, magically.
All I can do is to sit a while with
you in thought, word and deed.
If you need me, call.
Call and call. I shall be there.
We are lifeboats for each other.
Rough waters make gloom seem
deep, enveloping all potential.
Nevertheless some calmer seas
may come when least expected
or through the unlikely soul
who pops up in some quiet hour.
Hold on. Hold on.
Hope is still alive.
Hold on.

# On Placing a Loved One into Care

If you have done all you can the time
that you dreaded all along has come.
Know now that it is right to release your
individual to a wider circle of love.
Relax in the knowledge that this new stage
in life will never be perfect, but it can be
contented with peace of mind and soul.
No choice is neat or has to be permanent
even after all your research and thought.
There are reports and ratings to help validate
the kindness that can be sensed or seen
through an hand outstretched or a hug
anticipated for your Beloved or yourself.

# And Finally …

The following meditations are intended to help through the darkest days of grief. They are by no means complete or expert, just an offering from my soul to yours. I have taken many funeral services and have sat with families whose lives have been excoriated. There have been many occasions when I just wanted to cry with them and make everything better. In reality, the only thing I can do, is to be with them and provide as sincere a service as possible. For those few moments after meeting them, they become my family and we are connected eternally. What has consistently astonished me is how much hurt the human soul can endure. The way someone will come for a hug and hold onto you for just a moment longer than normal is as if our sheer proximity sustains their soul ~ it has sustained mine on many occasions..

When I go to a home where there has been a loss, I always feel it is an immense privilege to be allowed to share this part of their experience. The most important words that I can say, come at the beginning of our meeting when I ask, "What were the best things about your precious one?"

This question always leads to smiles, everyone leaps to say something positive with an affectionate pride. As we talk more about someone who has had led their life well, it is amazing just what is revealed: endearing and entertaining anecdotes layered with admiration. Within those tales are subtle nuances that reveal their personality, character and soul, are often only visible to the closest connections within families. When we share these insights, the whole community benefits because we all grow from listening to lessons from a special soul.

There has been one consistent theme throughout all of these interactions ~ the intensity of what a loyal and loving relationship can generate. Each experience and family is unique and they all want for their beloved to be recognised for their great worth. They want me to give a eulogy that captures the essence of a character who was kind, brave and funny ~ it's always about values and attitudes and never about worldly things.

When I can say lovely things about someone, it is because they have spent a lifetime being lovely. Every time we hear something good, we always have the choice to emulate that goodness. We best honour our loved ones when we carry on in the same tone or we can make things a little better. A small resolution can have significant influence in our world and help assuage some of those hard hours.

After one particularly tragic death of a young person, I was the last one at the graveside and waited until everyone had left. As I walked back to my car in a state of exhausted distress, I heard one of the best sounds in the world. There was a group of children on their bikes watching me in my cassock and started giggling at the sight of me fighting to keep the wind from lifting me up like Mary Poppins. The sheer folly of my appearance with their lovely laughter helped me greatly that morning.

There is a silent set of stars who help make a service special. A good funeral director will take care of everything to make things seamless. Their dignity and demeanour are assets to us all. Staff in Crematoria and cemeteries are highly organised and often provide a depth of kindness that no one ever sees. Things just quietly occur to make our transitions as comfortable as possible.

One of my lifejoy lectures is entitled, "How to have a fantastic funeral." It is not about how lavish or eccentric the service can be, it is about embracing all that life offers us so that the eulogy is a golden tapestry of relishing and cherishing all the gifts life offers us. The way to have a fantastic funeral is to have a fantastic life, a life full of compassion, contribution and courage. This book was designed to help you help yourself to have the best life possible, whatever our circumstances or challenges.

# Beyond Measure

I loved you beyond measure.
I will go on loving you.
My darling, I am so proud of you
of how you lived and loved.
I am trying to keep your
light alive in my days
and hours when I know
that I was blessed to
know and grow with you.
Thank you for being mine.
I long for one more
minute together.
I know it will come.
Wait for me.

# Loss of a Beloved

My soul aches for you whilst you are gone.
Too early from me, this makes no sense,
there is only pain. Such intensity must
prove how much I admired and cared.
Please know that if this were the measure of
devotion, you were worthy of it all.
I count the days until
we are together again when your
hand sits in mine and we laugh
at ourselves and watch the  world go by.
Now I trudge on searching and suffering,
I trust you are soaring,
which comforts me beyond compare.
Go gently my Beloved.
You are my hope.

# Birthday of a Loved One

Another year has passed so quickly
that I can hardly breathe for loving you.
Remembering the joy on those special
days but once a year is not enough to
celebrate all that was you.
I wonder how you would be now in this grand
age, like me? Wrinkled and grey yet young inside?
Inside, inside that is where you are
ageless and free and always with me.

# After a Good Marriage

I have spent a lifetime loving you,
before that there was only me.
I was merely waiting for us, just us.
Thank God for the unity we shared and loved.
Look at what we created, a net of souls
that have your spark of care, grace and beauty.
I see you everywhere in everything and everyone.
I am doing my best to make you proud of me,
to cope and survive and pray to thrive again.
And as the world carries on, know that I carry
you in every breath, thought and word.
Your lifetime was for loving me,
with my lifetime for loving you.

# Loss of Your Infant

From the first thought of you, I knew I loved you.
Your tiny being came from my soul
and into our world. I have never known such joy.
You were the purpose of my life and now you are
gone yet my purpose seems stronger than ever.
For all you gave me, in that short spell of heaven
on earth holding you, has made me richer,
deeper and whole.
Somehow I must continue with the
privilege of being yours.
You loved me so well.
Always know, I go on loving you beyond measure.

# On Your Child's Birthday

The blessing of you came to us, so full of hope.
Your birthday was the best day of all my life.
I saw you shine in the fun of it all ~
in the mess, the cake and the gifts.
Now that joy is quietened my love grows louder in
the hope that you can hear or see
or feel how much our world needs you
still on this birthday and beyond.
So I recall and pray that your birthdays will be the
point where I know you are safe,
strong and singing in my soul
and keep being the best blessing of my life.

# I Keep Thinking

I keep thinking of things that
I must tell you or ask what to
do, even though you set and
sorted everything for me
before you went. Then the jolt
hits me like a jagged slab
almost crushing my soul:
it is up to me now to
decide and deliver on all our
responsibilities and activities.
I left it all to you for too long
because you were so strong,
my leader and I loved that.
Now finally, it's time for me
to be responsible for it all.
I hope you approve
of my efforts and mistakes.
I am trying for you and for us.

# Christian Hope

I hope, I believe, I trust
that you are with our Lord,
by the side of God in spirit
and in flesh at peace,
to dance with vigour.
All I pray for now is
deliverance from missing you.
I take sanctuary in knowing
that you truly lived a
life of devoted truth to
witness to all that was
good, pure and real.
I keep trying to do all
that you would so that when
our Lord deems prudent,
I may join you and rejoice like
never before in the welcome that awaits.
I hope, I believe, I know.

# Homeward to Heaven

So the best hope, is that you're sitting with
Jesus, Gandhi, Van Gogh and Great Granny
in your idea of heaven.
For me it would be endless swimming and caravans
with a big fish supper and dark chocolate.
I know yours will feature footy and a shed.
Everyone is missing you intensely, such a shame you
didn't realise just how much you were loved ~ all those
lovely things they said at the funeral and beyond.
You're in a load of souls and minds and hearts which is
a life well lived. And now you coax and hope they make
good choices in kindness to build a legacy as rich as
yours and know how precious every hour can be.
I feel you're my angel so I'd better watch, listen and
learn to be my own best hope to sit with Jesus.

# Conclusions?

Thank you for picking up this offering and for the time we have spent together. I hope you found some vibrancy and valour in the words and between the lines. This was meant to be a celebration of humanity whilst not shying away from the very real challenges we all face. Everything was written to possess something that was pure in order to allow everyone an expression of their spirituality.

This was intended to address the spectrum from the devout to the doubter. Whatever you think, believe or know, always remember that questioning makes us stronger. Indeed, being inbetween is a lovely place in which to reside. A seeker is the soul trying to make sense of our world. Anyone who is certain about their faith or lack of it is often clinging to sureties that don't really exist. A bit of a dilemma about what we believe can have a great dignity to it when we allow ourselves to be open to the vast possibilities that lie within us.

Wherever we are in our lives, please know that there is always room for more excitement, wonder and adoration. If today is hard for you, hold on or reach out for someone and know that tomorrow may be a little brighter. The little exercises in this book were designed to help secure our foundations to enable us to be flexible enough to fly and grounded enough to cope. If you haven't started them yet or need some time to think, then please come back to them. They might just save your life and make your life. The final and most important offering in this book is to write a list of all those that love you, all the good things in your life and all of your accomplishments. When things are written down they become evidence which can be used in the case for our lifejoy. Keep adding to it, keep contributing and keep shining. We've come a long way together and the final exercise is Lifejoy empowerment at its best!

# Motivation is What We Need!

Motivation is one of those rare commodities in life where the more you have the better! It can transform the miserable to the mundane; the mundane to the marvellous and the marvellous to the miraculous. Excuses are not attractive; initiative and progress enable your light to shine so that your abilities can be appreciated. When I meet a new client for Life-Coaching this is the first exercise we undertake. It's fun, come on, get a nice pen and start ...

My Brilliant and Beautiful Blessings ~ Great and Small ...

1.

2.

3.

4.

5.

My Most Marvellous Accomplishments

1.

2.

3.

4.

5.


If you would like to book a Lifejoy Lecture, training or coaching session then please look at www.lifejoy.co We are looking forward to hearing from you. Be glorious, be your own lifejoy and pass it on …

God Bless, Oceans of love, Becca xxx

If you would like to book Dr Rebecca for a Lifejoy lecture, workshop or coaching session then please get in touch. For a free Lifejoy newsletter sign up at www.lifejoy.co and like us on Facebook and follow @DrDinsdale on twitter.

# Your  Lifejoy Lectures

"Lifejoy ~ A Serenity Spa for Your Soul."

"Whatever ~ How to Revise and Shine."

"Potential ~ Power-Up Your Motivation and Morale."

"Resurgam ~ How to Survive and Thrive through Adversity."

"Guesthouses do get Painted ~ How to be an Optimistic Realist."

"Oration ~
How to Speak in Public with Elegant Ease for Life and Work."

"Brainbox ~
A Swot Analysis to Enable Your Education and Employability."

"Heroic Hope ~
How the Northern Ireland Peace Process can Inspire You."

"Orange, Green and In Between ~
The Irish in the North-East of England."

"Mentor ~
What's the French for Entrepreneur? Insights for Business Start-Ups."

"Ivy Madeline in Manchuria ~
Inspiration from my Gran, the Medical Missionary."

"Exclusions to Excellence ~
Tremendous Tales from the Headmaster's Daughter."

"Dynamite ~ Explosive Exhortations from my Great-Gran's Empire."

"How to be an Historian ~ Plots, Pleasures and Primary Sources."

"Declutter Divas ~ How to have a Tidy Mind, Life and Home."

"There's a Book in Us All ~ How to Write Yours."

"How to have a Big Fat Ethical Wedding."

"How to have a Fantastic Funeral."